# don't bury me here

# don't bury me here

## Paul Hiram Mozley III

**Wasteland Press**
Shelbyville, KY USA
www.wastelandpress.net

*don't bury me here*
by paul hiram mozley III



First Printing – April 2008
ISBN:  978-1-60047-189-6
cover photo by Rusty James
www.sinisterelite.com



Printed in the U.S.A.

table of contents

foreword

   words are not the end, they carry the idea-the cry. poetry outshines what seems apparent to men and reveals a special fabric in the heart of god- a thread of hope that binds all things together. when i write it is on impulse-like when you are driving across a high bridge at sundown  and see the light cutting through the clouds, breaking on the water and you want to take a picture but know that no picture would capture the moment-the feeling-the brilliance. yet you want to take it just the same, not so much to remember the colors and clouds but the feeling and hope that gave them life and touched you in that transcendent moment. these poems are times when i touched clouds and rivers and bridges in my life and passed beyond them. they are all triumph because they reached beyond the veil and secured something real. there is a master craftsman at work and my prayer is that his artistry is reflected in my poetry for i am his workmanship and he is my muse. i hope you find something of yourself in my prose and are encouraged to never settle but to chase after the dawn.


-paul hiram mozley III
-saturday afternoon march 2008

play me like a tired record
strung up in your proud collection
dust me with your rags and magic
listen for the hidden static
my message rings out
can you grab it
the needle's end
is all but tragic


there is a lion in my room
he looks through ancient hope
that no one
before or sense
could beat out of him

no one could take your hope
not with whips or words
nor friends who fled into the world
not with nails or wood or shameful scorn
it was a flame which burst
swallowing death
consuming the criminal
on your left


if i spread out the galaxy
breathing hue in every leaf
throwing colors into mystery
turning orbits into me
then i can sense the wayward turn
of a heart that tries to earn
my affection
when it's free

reflections of a broken man


light
breaks
upon my back
criss-cross silhouette
and
the soft stirring of those limbs outside
my window
moving like music
to an ancient rhythm
a sacred hymn
that was sung on the day the world began



a fixed point in this cosmic stirring


star of beauty
i spin emphatically
in celestial orbit of your heart
i am terrestrial
sold into this world
pull me out
your pool within
round 'n' round
the ripulets
of your slightest motion
displacing all
that can be seen
in the cosmos
or heard
in these silent movements

in riotous upbraiding
of perilous factions
you wielded your happiness
with outcasts in actions
that wrought condemnation
from the ugly brood of vipers
who could not see the road for heavy rain
and lack of windshield wipers




before you go


search deeply
quickly
for
something
to carry us through
until we see you
with throne and throngs
of worshippers renewed

no envelope


war has brokenout
our borders are unprotected
raiders pillage and burn
spreading their spoils
on the unborn
reeking their havoc
in the high court
a call to action
and we're alarmed
that someone should shout
in the house of god


my heart just opened up
it was closed for years
for fears that disrupt
prodded me into darkness
probing me for confessions
now my torturers have vanished
like my dark obsessions
into light and glory strong
i lift my countenance to god
believing him to be the one
who split this adam with his holy love

# the call

what is to be said of freedom
who will herald his coming
will any stand with him
will all of us be running
away from the one we thought we were pursuing
live for his cause
take up his standard
carry his cross
carry his banner
defy the great hordes
take up the mantle
let his body arise
and prepare for battle
stand in his name
watch your enemies scatter
rise from your graves
go trim your lanterns
for the bridegroom is coming into his chamber
to awaken a love that has waited for ages
for all to be one work of salvation
you've been ransomed from death into his kingdom
now what is to be said of freedom

shackletown


she used to scrape our streets
for loose change
before she had reason to want anything
before she caught wind
of a descending trend
that stole her last bit of pride
the peril of wisdom
they sought it  she sold it
for one tenth of the price
a piece of forever that cost her
                                        her life
she went on to tell us that no man
had the right
to barter her promise
or pawn something like
this alabaster vial
she poured out tonight
        -               on
        -               that man

it was fear
that caught her unawares
when he reached for the thing that brought her here
touching the burning her shackles dislodged
no amount of searching could give her heart pause
till now
rejection disarmed
accusers cast down
no words but i love you
and no stain on her gown

the human remains


neath facades
of industrious weatherstrip
lies a
cataclysmic unknown
explorers
probing the great abyss
discover
betrayed lover
warm embraces
conjure images and faces
sent spiraling for cover
fragments of another world
where memories cling to dust
cloaking mystery in failure
separating us
-yet amid all these things
remains
one bright facet
glimmering at dawn
in subtle happenings
hopes ceaseless song
rising in the echo chamber
of lovelost and far flung
rushing past idols
deaf and dumb
to the throne of god

jesus,
look at me
trembling
slipping through the minute
opening
down the cylindrical figure
of the hourglass
into your sympathy




she is only pain
i would not throw myself into her
not for anything
not her deep
    blue eyes
not for long glances in fading light
not for the honor of walking her through
layers of images  mirrors  and lies
no
she is only pain

these memories
are mine
once tainted
restored
shake well
the darkness
coming to light
coming to focus
images surface
an emotional circus
i open the earth with
driving my stake in time
declaring
these memories
are mine




she will
be remembered
as twilight december
a lark
a sunburst
a woman
leftover fragments
become a poem
memories deplete
all my awareness
is spilled in the street
i move to another
more resplendent cause
shouting his name
lifting my arms
no longer afraid
of who i've become

born
then marred by disdain
one strong hand
changing channels
the other pushing me away
i run for cover
making my bed
on a pile of rubble
underneath an underpass
i feel my comfort will not last
rain has come
and soaked my house
tape dissolved  cardboard fell
drifting down the river now
i have no means to fish things out


throughout
the great flood
i wandered
in caverns
to span time
i ran backwards
into my youth
before the birth
of my failure
to become one pure sunset
in the heart of my father

save the one which never lived


would anyone stop me
if i threw my body to the street
if sweet and pain
walked a thousand miles
of earth and rain
and wound up on a street corner
in south dakota
throwing myself to the wind
scattering my imagined past
to see if i come back again


fourteen days


thoughts of traveling out alone
into his streets and alleys
losing my soul
i should pay attention
there is a war
i'm involved
i take shots
i went to a funeral
he drove off into a field alone
died in his car
everybody knows
he lost hope

to all of those with happy homes


i walked passed you
we shuffled four feet in the street
my eyes were downcast
so i saw your shoes
absorbing the impact
i noticed your wife
your children
your happy existence
i walked passed
life sojourns down an awkward path
i reach for things and put them back
i sense death too much
i feel pain/ so what
the world is a wound


religion


i fell asleep in my box
my feet are cold
because my socks
became my pillow
i can't swallow
the stench of the street
the pressure
of unwashed things
i have my alley
it's dark like me
never clean
never clean
it's
never clean

don't bury me here
carry my body
to the graves of my fathers
surround me with heroes
cold contrast of flowers
pale concrete
and
the thousand-yard stare
shouting orders like madmen
into the fear I might fail
rushing headlong to bullets
that rip through the air
tearing dreams from my helmet
and holes in my gear
i heard a faint whisper
don't bury me here


a man for no reason


that thick shadow
covered your soul
with raw displeasure
your familiar role
the constant subjecter
of the lesser
trees giving way to roads
frightened huddled masses
cowering in their complacent pose
so all the world can know
you were born
out of season
like a scarecrow in the dessert
a man for no reason

i refuse to carry this burden any longer
i will throw myself upon it
and die a thousand times familiar
to reach that hope beyond all hope
and leave confusion to the scholar


the future
leans heavy toward some great adventure
everything rushing to the epicenter
the earth is shaking
walls are crashing
inside my heart
i can't stop asking
that this be the final
forever conclusion
that this valley be flooded
with sunshine and music

as for me and my friends
we look to the future
with expectation
coming together
in the house of the ransomed
souls which piece
their lives together
into a dance
        a fire
        a spectrum
shinning forever
in every direction




we have outgrown our cover

we wrestle
tearing holes in the atmosphere
rifts appear
in twin realities
with varying degrees
of frequency
unlocking
subtle shades of mystery
as angelic beings
collect humble offerings
turning them into a breeze
 a fragrance spinning
through me
bouncing off
the outer ring
and
landing at your feet

director's cut

an arena
where
obscene onlookers with unsettled eye
gaze upon the praying one
till he rip and tear into another atmosphere
the curtain is thrown back
the universe revealed
light shines forth in triumphant array
                              of unwavering faith
bereft of disguise
his transparent heart hollows the lies
ferocious mouths are stopped for a time
while innocence stands somewhere outside
                    of itself
          with no need to be held
          his strength has arrived
          in the person of christ




eyes
hands
heart
marred
now married to god
redemption spreads
as you lift your head
woman-where are your accusers now

i don't have to live this way
there is a power which breaks
          soul barriers
lifting a life truculent
          to warrior
proposing a dream
so preposterous it seems
to come   from one
beyond these things
behind a veil
what remains
is found and held
by those who yield
to the truth
that
they must die to themselves


arms of christ

snared in barb-wire fence
wandering from the fold
fitting in alone
empathy in his approach
gravity   in his hope
tender hands
taking great pains
cleansing my soul
loosing my chains
i   became whole
he became home

i have run from pain
so far away
   i embraced
a deeper wound
   i faced
an empty tomb
and then a revelation
he is not here
he has ascended
not alone
he took my pain with him




temple


great fire
of indwelling spirit
pervasive movement
unflinching confidence
to stride in
diffusing a fragrance
compelling worship
no locked doors
no reinforced walls
i'm open
as you enter
your temple

no strings attached


i strummed my guitar
no sound came forth
alone in my room
the door locked
an invisible audience
i turned my back
he said i want your music
no strings attached


to grieve a loss
to mourn because
a soul burdened must find some repose
a wound must close
to heal
i am not a man of steel
but flesh and bone
when i bend
        i break
once i'm broken   it's over
no more lingering delusions to offer
a piece of me holds life eternal
and the god of all says
that is why i've come
the wounded healer

calloused
cold   cracked
bleeding
scrapes
scars  splinters
bleeding
they came to me reluctantly
as the son of a carpenter
i never wanted them
now they are my hands
beating the air
furious and real
as the earth beneath my nails




my hands are cold
mid-november
callous clutch of winter
sliding down my neck
raking across my sweet
into my flesh
like splinters

since they're new


i'll try them on
walk around a bit
see how they feel
do they grip the terrain
move unrestrained
respond to the way i feel everyday
or do they have an agenda
promote propaganda
spinning their confusion
around my watchtower
on this
the darkest afternoon




metronome


one light blinks
another rushes past
softly
in pale reflection
i sense my deepest thoughts
untouched
on pane of glass

i see you
crouched in corner
cowering as if some unresolved conflict
may strike you unawares
the moment
you crack
a smile


cynical
is a coat
you wear against the weather
critical
is the tongue
binding your thoughts together
with unflinching resolution
in the face
of what will come
steady yourself friend
for the wind blows
on everyone

hey
i remember you
late hours typing
reaching for fame
in one grandiose lame
attempt
to sidestep
the torrent of shame
that cascades
like so many movements of shade
through the blinds
until the time
the sun retreats to palisades
on the other side of things
where dormant accolades
adorn the walls
and flood the caves
with clues
for future generations
made to scrape the dust
from the awkward line that must
have been scrawled
by a neanderthal
with a ladder
tall enough
to see
inside
the heart of the matter

one last  lament


my cold dinner plate
rest on the arm
of our green couch
i want you
to come
and take it out
to do something for me
i can easily do myself




she whispers to the wounded
prayers for the downtrodden ones
who wander into her yard
disoriented and lost
grace gives them what they want
loosing them from what hurts
receiving us into her heart
            into quiet
                peace
                and god

all my friends at the orphanage
talk about their parents
how one day they'll come for them
        one day there will be a big full house
of sounds and smells and rooms
to laugh and play and do the things
orphans never do
gentle words to tuck you in
strong arms to raise you up
and when the first day of school begins
to take you to the bus
to close your eyes and drift away
before the terror starts
looming over every feeling
tainting every thought
a deeper melancholy
known by those
whose parents are their hurt

i have seen
joy dispelled
light gave out
shadows fell
into the recess of the fog
incessant noise
burning heart
all my efforts to retreat
where stifled in the rising heat
incense in an empty room
sweet and pain my perfume
pouring out as i dance
far from sorrows cruel grasp
into a creed that binds all things
while stars of mourning rise to sing
beautiful are your feet
the only place where i find peace


she doesn't do well with names
places/things
hurrying unseen
always inbetween
wrestling
under covers
for the sanctity that smothers
her voice
in a collapsing void
of pretense
noise
and explosive moments
where she resembles her mother

my eyes are closed
my dreams are close
i feel an impulse
and let it go

time is slipping by
speeding up
spill it out
on those you love

words for seeds to spurn their growth
wind to come and carry hope
across the plains and down the road
a light remains for us to know
these clouds will break and call us home

she dances for me
her face haunted by pain
a long shadow in her smile
that her eyes betray
she clothes herself in shame
for a dollar bill
crumpled and old
like a weary traveler
trying to get home
i sit for awhile watching the show
falling in love with a ghost


some of my best thoughts come
when i am outside
unfettered
rythmatic inclin-
nation
to observe
the inscription
on the sky
to loose myself
from the cares that bind
my heart
in general time
and meaningless task
which produce frustration
and never last
because their made of plastic
and i am of grass


paul hiram mozley III – 31

of all the joys
i think you best
the power you posses
to turn a heart like this
to blaze
when not so many days
ago
i was agape
with wounds and woe
your song in dark hours arose
lifting me from the throes
a soul restored
a child wanted
despite my imperfect performance
and the charge against me so enormous


life


swell of synergy
centripetal force
rising from nothing
to take down the curse
hands fluid motion
feet will not rest
till my lips taste the passion
inside this hot kiss

soon


this long walk
across
my twenties
has prepared me
for love
i will find you in a morning valley
before the coming of the dawn
and the blade of our young love
is forged in the fire
of our finding each other



soft
compelling
deep understanding
anxious
hands reaching
lips touching
hearts blending
eyes meeting
both knowing
being known
becoming one
becoming home

a month of summer


too easy
too late
come closer
wait
my lover
takes
forever
i take
summer
and strum her
homespun chords
on my guitar
until
a song is born
that turns my heart to warm
and spirit calm
like the dandelions praying
in my front yard




lucy


dance
      while you can
sing
      and raise your hands
run with streamers
into hearts forever winter
spreading sunshine as you enter

one brave flower
resplendent in the sun
dragonflies dancing
because that is what their made of
wind from a distant storm
whispers to me
that these
are the days of my life
and this
is what their made of


i ran on the beach last night
i sprinted
from i do not know what
to i do not know where
until
i got there

oh- the release
words bring
when found covering
some aged hurt
inflicted by a careless world
they hit me
but did not disturb
my innermost and final verse

about the author


Paul is a traveler, musician, student and poet. He writes what he sees and feels what he writes. His poetry is honest, terse and hopeful. He currently makes his living in marine construction in Virginia Beach, VA, where he is pursuing a degree in religious studies. To contact him, check out: www.myspace.com/paulionprolificproductions

9 781600 471896